SUMMER OLYMPIC LEGENDS

TRACK & FIELD

BY SHANE FREDERICK

CREATIVE EDUCATION

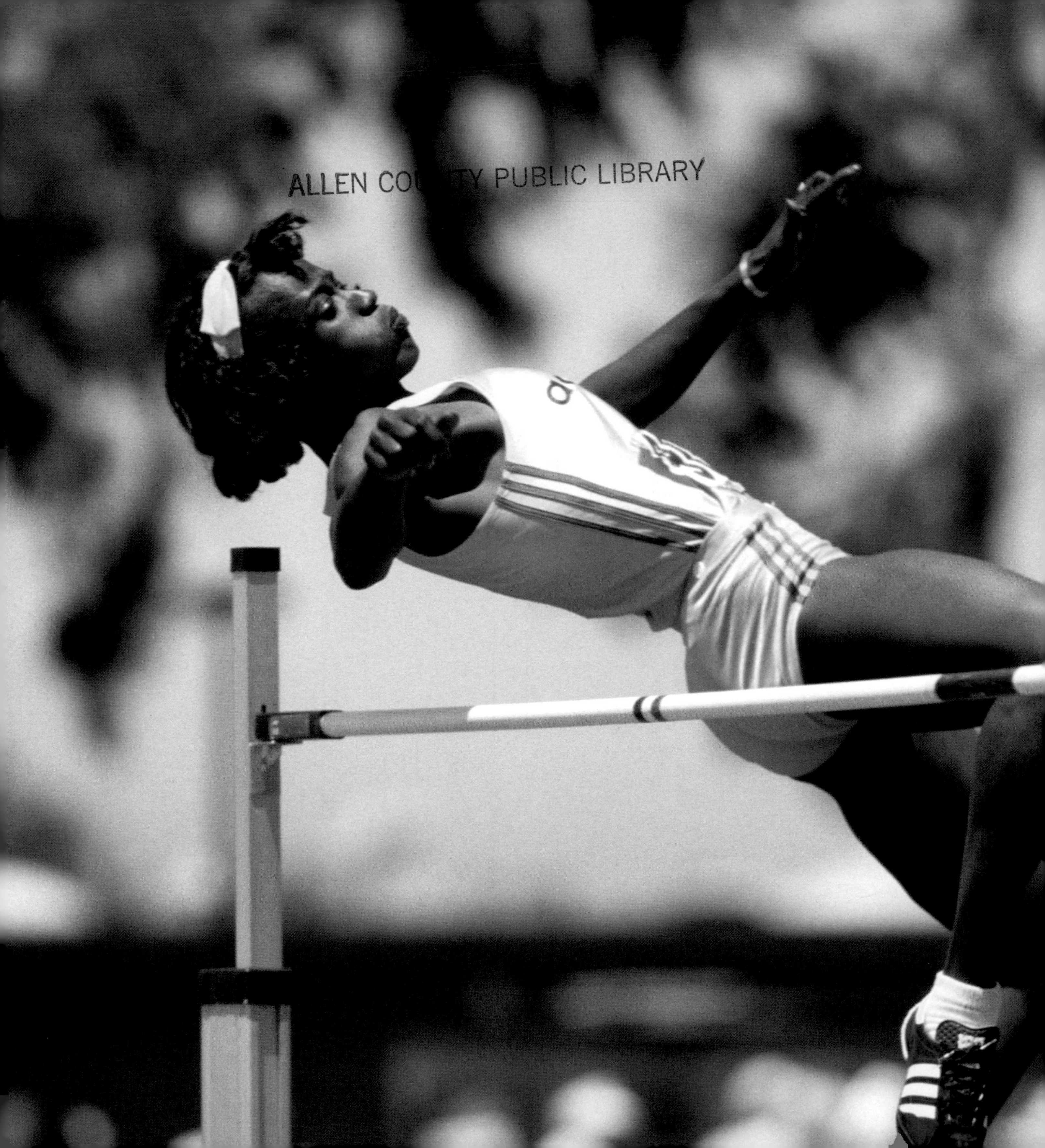

CONTENTS

INTRODUCTION

Throughout human history, people have always sought to challenge themselves, to compete against others, and to discover the limits of their capabilities. Such desires can turn destructive, leading to war. But the ancient Greeks also recognized the good in these human traits, and it was because of them that the Olympic Games—featuring running races, jumping contests, throwing competitions, and wrestling and boxing matches—began more than 2,700 years ago. The ancient Olympics ended in A.D. 393, but the Games were revived in 1896 in hopes of promoting world peace through sports. Fittingly, the first "modern" Olympics were held in Athens, Greece, but they moved around the world every four years after that. In 2009, it was announced that the Games would be held in South America for the first time, going to Rio de Janeiro, Brazil, in 2016.

Every 1896 Olympian received a medal reading "International Olympic Games, Athens 1896"

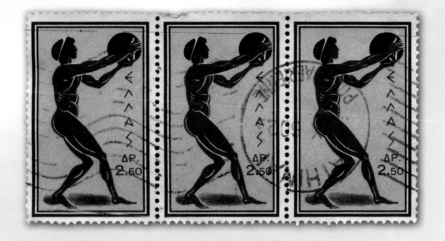

One of the most exciting sports in the Olympics has always been track and field, otherwise known as athletics. The history of athletics dates back to the original Greek Games. Many of the same events have carried over from ancient times to today, from sprinting and distance running on the track, to long and high jumping, to the throwing of **discuses**, shots, and **javelins**. During the 1896 Summer Games, there were only a dozen events in track and field, and 63 men (no women) from 11 countries competed against each other. But 112 years later, during the 2008 Olympics in Beijing, China, more than 2,000 men and women from 200 countries were running, leaping, or throwing for gold in 47 athletics events.

Throughout the history of the Olympics, some of the most exciting and memorable moments have taken place inside the giant, jam-packed stadiums built around the world for track and field. This is where Wilma Rudolph, Bob Beamon, and Usain Bolt stunned big crowds by shattering world records. It's where Al Oerter, Carl Lewis, and Jackie Joyner-Kersee showed off their mighty arms and fleet feet and collected numerous medals. And it's where Dorando Pietri, Rafer Johnson, and Derek Redmond demonstrated that— sometimes—a big heart is the most important muscle an Olympian can have.

The ancient Greeks celebrated human achievement and the human form, with athletes competing nude

1896 ATHENS, GREECE

1900 PARIS, FRANCE

1904 ST. LOUIS, MISSOURI

1908 LONDON, ENGLAND

1912 STOCKHOLM, SWEDEN

1920 ANTWERP, BELGIUM

1924 PARIS, FRANCE

1928 AMSTERDAM, NETHERLANDS

1932 LOS ANGELES, CALIFORNIA

1936 BERLIN, GERMANY

1948 LONDON, ENGLAND

1952 HELSINKI, FINLAND

1956 MELBOURNE, AUSTRALIA

1960 ROME, ITALY

1964 TOKYO, JAPAN

1968 MEXICO CITY, MEXICO

1972 MUNICH, WEST GERMANY

1976 MONTREAL, QUEBEC

1980 MOSCOW, SOVIET UNION

1984 LOS ANGELES, CALIFORNIA

1988 SEOUL, SOUTH KOREA

1992 BARCELONA, SPAIN

1996 ATLANTA, GEORGIA

2000 SYDNEY, AUSTRALIA

2004 ATHENS, GREECE

2008 BEIJING, CHINA

2012 LONDON, ENGLAND

THE GREAT RACE

1908 LONDON, ENGLAND

The first three modern Olympic Games were not very successful. They took place in Athens, Greece; Paris, France; and St. Louis, Missouri. But getting the best athletes in the world together in those great cities proved to be difficult before the age of air travel, and fans were not very interested in the new competition.

Dorando Pietri was disqualified from the 1908 marathon, but his effort made him an international star

That all changed in 1908 in London, England. The excitement and drama that people have come to expect in the Olympics every four years can be traced back to those Games—and to, specifically, the men's marathon (there was no women's race). Athletes ran the long-distance race in the first three Olympics, but the London Games established what would become the official distance of 26.2 miles that still is used today.

On a hot July 24, 1908, crowds gathered in the streets from **Windsor Castle** to White City Stadium to witness the 55 runners from around the world who took on the demanding course. Inside the stadium, nearly 100,000 waited for the dramatic finish. Once the competitors entered the arena, they had to run 385 yards—the extra two-tenths of a mile—to the finish line, which was placed in front of the British royal family's viewing box. Dorando Pietri of Italy was the first to enter the stadium. He had a one-minute lead on his closest competitor, American John J. Hayes. But the Italian was exhausted due to the heat and took a wrong turn on the track. After realizing his error and turning around, Pietri could barely run, and he collapsed five times.

"The man was practically delirious," one reporter wrote. "He staggered along the **cinder** path like a man in a dream, his **gait** being neither a walk nor a run, but simply a flounder, with arms shaking and legs tottering."

Each time Pietri fell, Olympic officials helped him back to his feet. They assisted him to the finish line, making sure that he was on his feet as he hit the line just as Hayes was entering the stadium. The American circled the track and finished the marathon 32 seconds behind Pietri. The United States protested the outcome, arguing that Pietri received help, which was against the rules.

Pietri was disqualified, and Hayes received the gold medal as the winner. The Italian, who was taken to a hospital after the race, didn't leave the Olympics empty-handed, however. His determination to finish the race won him many fans, including Britain's Queen Alexandra, who presented him with a silver cup as a reward for his gallant effort.

World-Record Marathon Times
1908 John J. Hayes 2:55:18
2011 Patrick Makau 2:03:38

ATHENS, GREECE	PARIS, FRANCE	ST. LOUIS, MISSOURI	LONDON, ENGLAND	STOCKHOLM, SWEDEN	ANTWERP, BELGIUM	PARIS, FRANCE	AMSTERDAM, NETHERLANDS	LOS ANGELES, CALIFORNIA	BERLIN, GERMANY	LONDON, ENGLAND	HELSINKI, FINLAND	MELBOURNE, AUSTRALIA	ROME, ITALY	TOKYO, JAPAN	MEXICO CITY, MEXICO	MUNICH, WEST GERMANY	MONTREAL, QUEBEC	MOSCOW, SOVIET UNION	LOS ANGELES, CALIFORNIA	SEOUL, SOUTH KOREA	BARCELONA, SPAIN	ATLANTA, GEORGIA	SYDNEY, AUSTRALIA	ATHENS, GREECE	BEIJING, CHINA	LONDON, ENGLAND
1896	1900	1904	1908	1912	1920	1924	1928	1932	1936	1948	1952	1956	1960	1964	1968	1972	1976	1980	1984	1988	1992	1996	2000	2004	2008	2012

THE MULTI-SPORT STAR

JIM THORPE U.S. EVENTS: DECATHLON, PENTATHLON OLYMPIC COMPETITION: 1912

Jim Thorpe was known as the world's greatest athlete for the first half of the 20th century. An American Indian from Oklahoma, he was a college football star in the early days of the sport and later played professional football and baseball. His college football coach, the famous **Pop Warner**, hyped Thorpe as "the greatest all-around athlete in the world." But it was during the 1912 Olympics

Jim Thorpe (above) was celebrated in such movies as 1951's Jim Thorpe: All-American (opposite)

8

> **"He was the greatest athlete who ever lived."** – *Abel Kiviat*

in Stockholm, Sweden, that Thorpe truly earned this distinguished title.

That summer, Thorpe entered the Games in two events—the pentathlon and the decathlon—that each consisted of multiple **disciplines**. The pentathlon featured five competitions in one day, and Thorpe won four of them on his way to the gold medal. He took first in the long jump, discus, 200-meter dash, and 1,500-meter run. He finished third in the javelin throw despite never having seen a javelin until just a few weeks before the Olympics. "He was the greatest athlete who ever lived," said Thorpe's Olympic teammate, Abel Kiviat, a silver medalist in the 1,500. "What he had was natural ability. There wasn't anything he couldn't do. All he had to see is someone doing something and he tried it … and he'd do it better."

Up next for Thorpe was the decathlon. This time it was 10 events over 3 days, but this increased workload was still no problem. Thorpe placed first in four events—the 1,500-meter run, 110-meter hurdles, high jump, and **shot put**—and he finished

third or fourth in the others (javelin, pole vault, discus, long jump, 400-meter dash, and 100-meter dash). The decathlon scoring system, which has changed slightly over the years, awards points in each event based on a predetermined formula. Thorpe's effort not only won him another gold medal, but it also set a world points record that stood for almost 20 years.

In 15 events in the decathlon and pentathlon, Jim Thorpe won 8 of them. During the closing ceremonies, Sweden's king, Gustav V, said to Thorpe, "You, sir, are the greatest athlete in the world. I would consider it an honor to shake your hand." The soft-spoken Thorpe replied, "Thanks, King."

The 1912 Games were the only ones in which Thorpe competed. A year later, it was discovered that he had played minor-league baseball for pay prior to becoming an Olympian. Because professionals were not allowed to compete in the Olympics then, Thorpe's medals and records were taken away from him. It wasn't until 1982—almost 30 years after his death—that the International Olympic Committee (IOC) proclaimed Thorpe the winner again and presented replicas of his medals to his children.

ATHENS, GREECE 1896
PARIS, FRANCE 1900
ST. LOUIS, MISSOURI 1904
LONDON, ENGLAND 1908
STOCKHOLM, SWEDEN 1912
ANTWERP, BELGIUM 1920
PARIS, FRANCE 1924
AMSTERDAM, NETHERLANDS 1928
LOS ANGELES, CALIFORNIA 1932
BERLIN, GERMANY 1936
LONDON, ENGLAND 1948
HELSINKI, FINLAND 1952
MELBOURNE, AUSTRALIA 1956
ROME, ITALY 1960
TOKYO, JAPAN 1964
MEXICO CITY, MEXICO 1968
MUNICH, WEST GERMANY 1972
MONTREAL, QUEBEC 1976
MOSCOW, SOVIET UNION 1980
LOS ANGELES, CALIFORNIA 1984
SEOUL, SOUTH KOREA 1988
BARCELONA, SPAIN 1992
ATLANTA, GEORGIA 1996
SYDNEY, AUSTRALIA 2000
ATHENS, GREECE 2004
BEIJING, CHINA 2008
LONDON, ENGLAND 2012

THE FLYING FINN

PAAVO NURMI FINLAND EVENTS: 1,500-METER RUN, 5,000-METER RUN, 10,000-METER RUN, 3,000-METER STEEPLECHASE, 3,000-METER RUN (TEAM), CROSS-COUNTRY (INDIVIDUAL), CROSS-COUNTRY (TEAM) OLYMPIC COMPETITIONS: 1920, 1924, 1928

Paavo Nurmi always ran with a stopwatch. He didn't care what his competitors were doing on the track. He was worried only about his own pace and time. He knew what he needed to do to win. Everything else that was happening in the race was irrelevant. "When you race against time, you don't have to sprint," he once said. "Others can't hold the pace if it is steady and hard all through to the tape."

Paavo Nurmi (center) seldom spoke, letting his famously machinelike running pace do the talking

That was true throughout Nurmi's Olympic career. One day during the 1924 Olympics in Paris, France, Nurmi won the 1,500-meter run and set an Olympic record along the way. Less than 2 hours later, he was back at the starting line, this time for the 5,000 meters. Few distance runners today compete at both distances, and they certainly wouldn't run both races on the same day. But Nurmi was out there with his stopwatch. At some point late in the race, he checked his time, tossed the stopwatch into the grass, and picked up his pace. He went on to win another gold medal and set another Olympic record. "Mind is everything," Nurmi once said. "Muscle—pieces of rubber. All that I am, I am because of my mind."

Nurmi ran several distances and won at all of them. As a result, he was nicknamed "The Flying Finn" and "The King of Runners." As of 2011, he was one of only four Olympic athletes to have collected nine gold medals in a career. He also won 3 silver medals, and no track-and-field athlete has earned more medals than Nurmi's

total of 12. In the Paris Olympics alone, he won five golds. Besides the 1,500 and 5,000, he won the 10,000-meter cross-country race and led Finland to wins in the cross-country and 3,000-meter team races (long-distance team races no longer exist in Olympic competition).

Nurmi also won gold in the 10,000 meters in the 1920 Olympics in Antwerp, Belgium, and the 1928 Games in Amsterdam, Netherlands. A Finnish sports journalist wrote of Nurmi, "He conquered the world by pure means: with a will that had a supernatural power."

Paavo Nurmi's Gold Medals

Antwerp, 1920	10,000-meter run
	Cross-country (individual)
	Cross-country (team)
Paris, 1924	1,500-meter run
	5,000-meter run
	3,000-meter run (team)
	Cross-country (individual)
	Cross-country (team)
Amsterdam, 1928	10,000-meter run

1896 ATHENS, GREECE
1900 PARIS, FRANCE
1904 ST. LOUIS, MISSOURI
1908 LONDON, ENGLAND
1912 STOCKHOLM, SWEDEN
1920 ANTWERP, BELGIUM
1924 PARIS, FRANCE
1928 AMSTERDAM, NETHERLANDS
1932 LOS ANGELES, CALIFORNIA
1936 BERLIN, GERMANY
1948 LONDON, ENGLAND
1952 HELSINKI, FINLAND
1956 MELBOURNE, AUSTRALIA
1960 ROME, ITALY
1964 TOKYO, JAPAN
1968 MEXICO CITY, MEXICO
1972 MUNICH, WEST GERMANY
1976 MONTREAL, QUEBEC
1980 MOSCOW, SOVIET UNION
1984 LOS ANGELES, CALIFORNIA
1988 SEOUL, SOUTH KOREA
1992 BARCELONA, SPAIN
1996 ATLANTA, GEORGIA
2000 SYDNEY, AUSTRALIA
2004 ATHENS, GREECE
2008 BEIJING, CHINA
2012 LONDON, ENGLAND

OWENS DEFIES THE FÜHRER

1936 BERLIN, GERMANY

American sports fans knew the greatness of Jesse Owens before the 1936 Olympics in Berlin, Germany. A year earlier, while competing in track and field for Ohio State University, he dominated the Big Ten Conference championships in Michigan by setting 3 world records and tying a 4th in the span of about 45 minutes.

Once in Germany, however, Owens, an African American, wasn't treated as a champion. Nazi dictator Adolf Hitler wanted to use the Games as a way to prove to the world his belief that Aryans—white, European, non-Jewish people—were superior to all others. He expected the German athletes to dominate the Games. Hitler even called Owens and other black American

Jesse Owens explained his speed by saying, "I let my feet spend as little time on the ground as possible"

athletes "African **auxiliaries**," implying that they weren't full or legitimate members of the U.S. team. Owens was not fazed. "I wanted no part of politics," he said. "And I wasn't in Berlin to compete against any one athlete. The purpose of the Olympics, anyway, was to do your best. As I'd learned long ago from Charles Riley [his high school coach], the only victory that counts is the one over yourself."

Owens spoiled Hitler's show. He became the first American to win four gold medals in one Olympiad and set two world records along the way. Those records were in the 200-meter dash, which he finished in just 20.7 seconds, and as a member of the 4x100-meter relay team. He ran the first **leg** of the relay, and the U.S. team, which also included sprinters Ralph Metcalfe, Foy Draper, and Frank Wykoff, won in 39.8 seconds.

Owens blazed through the 100-meter dash in 10.3 seconds and set an Olympic record in the long jump with a leap of 26 feet, 5-½ inches. The electrifying Owens also won over the Olympic Stadium crowd, which cheered as he ran around the track, and found a fan in German long jumper Luz Long. Long, who even offered some advice before Owens's final, gold-winning jump, took the silver. Afterward, he congratulated Owens in front of the entire crowd, including the **führer** himself, Adolf Hitler. "It took a lot of courage for him to befriend me in front of Hitler," Owens later said. "You can melt down all the medals and cups I have and they wouldn't be a plating on the 24-karat friendship I felt for Luz Long at the moment. Hitler must have gone crazy watching us embrace."

Owens's performance in Berlin prompted many people to declare him the world's greatest athlete. Indeed, no other track-and-field athlete would win 4 gold medals in a single Olympics for another 48 years.

> **"[T]he only victory that counts is the one over yourself."** – *Jesse Owens*

ATHENS, GREECE 1896

PARIS, FRANCE 1900

ST. LOUIS, MISSOURI 1904

LONDON, ENGLAND 1908

STOCKHOLM, SWEDEN 1912

ANTWERP, BELGIUM 1920

PARIS, FRANCE 1924

AMSTERDAM, NETHERLANDS 1928

LOS ANGELES, CALIFORNIA 1932

BERLIN, GERMANY 1936

LONDON, ENGLAND 1948

HELSINKI, FINLAND 1952

MELBOURNE, AUSTRALIA 1956

ROME, ITALY 1960

TOKYO, JAPAN 1964

MEXICO CITY, MEXICO 1968

MUNICH, WEST GERMANY 1972

MONTREAL, QUEBEC 1976

MOSCOW, SOVIET UNION 1980

LOS ANGELES, CALIFORNIA 1984

SEOUL, SOUTH KOREA 1988

BARCELONA, SPAIN 1992

ATLANTA, GEORGIA 1996

SYDNEY, AUSTRALIA 2000

ATHENS, GREECE 2004

BEIJING, CHINA 2008

LONDON, ENGLAND 2012

A BLAZING TRAIL BLAZER

1948 LONDON, ENGLAND

In 1936 in Berlin, Germany, Fanny Blankers-Koen competed in her first Olympics. She failed to win a medal, but she came away with another prize: Jesse Owens's autograph. Owens won 4 gold

As a teenager, Fanny Blankers-Koen excelled at many sports, but she decided to apply herself to track

WEEK ENDING FEBRUARY 21 1948   EVERY WEDNESDAY THREEPENCE

ILLUSTRATED

MAUREEN'S A
CHAMPION

medals in those Games, and it was natural for the 18-year-old Dutch woman, who was also a sprinter, to want a **memento** from her idol.

The next two Olympics were cancelled because of World War II. Blankers-Koen became a star in international track and field, but the cancellations meant she didn't get a chance to go for another Olympic medal until she was 30 years old. In 1948 in London, England, Blankers-Koen was a mother of two, and some people thought she should not have left her family home in the Netherlands in order to run and jump in the Olympics. At the time, it was considered peculiar for a woman who was married with children to continue competing in sports.

But Blankers-Koen ignored the critics. She not only won gold, but she did what Owens had done in Berlin—claimed four gold medals. She reigned supreme in the 100-meter dash, the 200-meter dash, and the 80-meter hurdles, and she ran the anchor leg of the winning 4x100-meter relay team. "One newspaperman wrote that I was too old to run, that I should stay home and take care of my children," she said. "When I got to London, I pointed my finger at him and said, 'I show you.'" Blankers-Koen showed everyone, and her success earned her the nickname, "The Flying Housewife."

Blankers-Koen was also a tremendously successful jumper, setting world records in the high jump and the long jump in competitions in her home country of the Netherlands and at other meets throughout Europe. It's likely that she would have won medals in those events during the 1948 Olympics, but there was a rule at the time that prevented women from competing in more than three individual events.

Still, Blankers-Koen's success in those four events helped move women's competition into the spotlight. She was a star, which was confirmed when she encountered Owens for a second time several years later. "When I met him again in Munich at the 1972 Olympics, I said, 'I still have your autograph. I'm Fanny Blankers-Koen.' He said, 'You don't have to tell me who you are, I know everything about you.' Isn't that incredible? Jesse Owens knew who I was."

> **"One newspaperman wrote that I ... should stay home and take care of my children."** – *Fanny Blankers-Koen*

Blankers-Koen paved the way for other female stars such as British hurdler Maureen Gardner (pictured)

ATHENS, GREECE 1896
PARIS, FRANCE 1900
ST. LOUIS, MISSOURI 1904
LONDON, ENGLAND 1908
STOCKHOLM, SWEDEN 1912
ANTWERP, BELGIUM 1920
PARIS, FRANCE 1924
AMSTERDAM, NETHERLANDS 1928
LOS ANGELES, CALIFORNIA 1932
BERLIN, GERMANY 1936
LONDON, ENGLAND 1948
HELSINKI, FINLAND 1952
MELBOURNE, AUSTRALIA 1956
ROME, ITALY 1960
TOKYO, JAPAN 1964
MEXICO CITY, MEXICO 1968
MUNICH, WEST GERMANY 1972
MONTREAL, QUEBEC 1976
MOSCOW, SOVIET UNION 1980
LOS ANGELES, CALIFORNIA 1984
SEOUL, SOUTH KOREA 1988
BARCELONA, SPAIN 1992
ATLANTA, GEORGIA 1996
SYDNEY, AUSTRALIA 2000
ATHENS, GREECE 2004
BEIJING, CHINA 2008
LONDON, ENGLAND 2012

DOMINATING THE DISCUS

AL OERTER U.S. EVENT: DISCUS OLYMPIC COMPETITIONS: 1956, 1960, 1964, 1968

During the 1968 Olympics in Mexico City, many people considered American Jay Silvester to be the odds-on favorite to win the gold medal in the discus throw. He had set the world record earlier that summer in the U.S. Olympic Trials and had set the Olympic record in that week's **qualifying rounds**. But Silvester knew that the road to gold would not be so easy—Al Oerter was in the competition.

The legendary Al Oerter was a physical powerhouse, standing 6-foot-4 and weighing 280 pounds

"When you throw against Oerter," Silvester said, "you don't expect to win. You just hope."

Sure enough, Oerter bested Silvester and everybody else in the Olympic finals. He threw the discus a career-best 212 feet, 6 inches, even though he had a torn thigh muscle and was competing in heavy rain. It was Oerter's fourth gold medal in a row in the discus. At the time, no other track-and-field athlete had accomplished such a feat. *The New York Times* wrote: "At four-year intervals, the world is treated to 29 days in February, a United States presidential election, and Al Oerter winning an Olympic gold medal."

It was easy for the newspaper to look back and say that Oerter's wins were a given. But the truth was that Oerter was not favored to win any of his golds. In the 1956 Olympics in Melbourne, Australia, the 20-year-old surprised everyone by setting an Olympic record and upsetting the rest of the field. After recovering from a near fatal car accident, he did the same in the 1960 Games in Rome, Italy. Six days prior to the 1964 Games in Tokyo, Japan, Oerter injured himself while practicing, tearing **cartilage** in his ribcage. The injury caused **stabbing** pain with every throw, and doctors advised him to withdraw from the competition. Oerter refused. "These are the Olympics," he said. "You die for them." Of course, he went out, set another Olympic record, and won gold. "In the opinion of many of us, he is the greatest field-event athlete of the century," said American Harold Connolly, a gold medalist in the hammer throw. "There's a magic about him when he's competing."

Throwing a discus is deceptively difficult, as the perfect throw requires great spin and a precise trajectory

1896	1900	1904	1908	1912	1920	1924	1928	1932	1936	1948	1952	**1956**	**1960**	1964	1968	1972	1976	1980	1984	1988	1992	1996	2000	2004	2008	2012
ATHENS, GREECE	PARIS, FRANCE	ST. LOUIS, MISSOURI	LONDON, ENGLAND	STOCKHOLM, SWEDEN	ANTWERP, BELGIUM	PARIS, FRANCE	AMSTERDAM, NETHERLANDS	LOS ANGELES, CALIFORNIA	BERLIN, GERMANY	LONDON, ENGLAND	HELSINKI, FINLAND	MELBOURNE, AUSTRALIA	ROME, ITALY	TOKYO, JAPAN	MEXICO CITY, MEXICO	MUNICH, WEST GERMANY	MONTREAL, QUEBEC	MOSCOW, SOVIET UNION	LOS ANGELES, CALIFORNIA	SEOUL, SOUTH KOREA	BARCELONA, SPAIN	ATLANTA, GEORGIA	SYDNEY, AUSTRALIA	ATHENS, GREECE	BEIJING, CHINA	LONDON, ENGLAND

BEAUTY, GRACE, AND SPEED

WILMA RUDOLPH U.S. EVENTS: 100-METER DASH, 200-METER DASH, 4X100-METER RELAY OLYMPIC COMPETITIONS: 1956, 1960

Wilma Rudolph was just 16 years old and a high school junior when she competed in her first Olympics. The Tennessee native traveled to Melbourne, Australia, in 1956 to compete in two events. She didn't medal in the 200-meter dash, but she did help the United States' 4x100-meter relay team

Wilma Rudolph was a track sensation, with many people calling her "the fastest woman in history"

capture a bronze medal, running the third leg of the relay.

Four years later in Rome, Italy, Rudolph was a star. To friends and teammates, she was known as "Skeeter," a nickname given to her by her high school basketball coach because she was little and fast like a mosquito. But to those who witnessed her beauty, grace, and speed on the track, Rudolph earned other titles. Italians called her *La Gazella Nera*—"the Black Gazelle"—while the French called her *La Perle Noire*—"the Black Pearl."

The 1960 Games didn't start off well for Rudolph. The day before the 100-meter dash competition began, she stepped in a sprinkler hole during a warmup and twisted her ankle badly. She was afraid that she might not be able to race on the world's biggest stage. But the next day, Rudolph decided that she could run, and the injury never seemed to bother her for the rest of the Olympics. She tied the world record in the 100-meter semifinals, running the race in 11.3

Wilma Rudolph's Fastest Times
100-meter dash 11.0 seconds
200-meter dash 23.2 seconds

seconds. In the finals, Rudolph won the gold with a memorable time of 11 seconds flat. That would have been the world record if not for the heavy breeze blowing at the runners' backs that day. Ed Temple, Wilma's coach, couldn't believe that she had won with her bad ankle. He couldn't see the finish line from where he was standing and was told about her win. "You're joking," he said. "[Then] they flashed it on the big scoreboard and put the time, the new Olympic record, 'Wilma Rudolph USA,' and I said, 'Hot Dog!'"

The next event was the 200, the sprint Rudolph had struggled with in Melbourne. But it was her best event, and this time, she didn't disappoint. After setting an Olympic record in the first **heat** with a time of 23.2 seconds, she went on to capture the gold medal. Rudolph became the first American woman to win three gold medals in the Olympics when she ran the anchor leg and helped the 4x100 team to a first-place finish. "She was the Jesse Owens of women's track and field," Olympic historian Bud Greenspan said, "and like Jesse, she changed the sport for all time."

ATHENS, GREECE	PARIS, FRANCE	ST. LOUIS, MISSOURI	LONDON, ENGLAND	STOCKHOLM, SWEDEN	ANTWERP, BELGIUM	PARIS, FRANCE	AMSTERDAM, NETHERLANDS	LOS ANGELES, CALIFORNIA	BERLIN, GERMANY	LONDON, ENGLAND	HELSINKI, FINLAND	MELBOURNE, AUSTRALIA	ROME, ITALY	TOKYO, JAPAN	MEXICO CITY, MEXICO	MUNICH, WEST GERMANY	MONTREAL, QUEBEC	MOSCOW, SOVIET UNION	LOS ANGELES, CALIFORNIA	SEOUL, SOUTH KOREA	BARCELONA, SPAIN	ATLANTA, GEORGIA	SYDNEY, AUSTRALIA	ATHENS, GREECE	BEIJING, CHINA	LONDON, ENGLAND
1896	1900	1904	1908	1912	1920	1924	1928	1932	1936	1948	1952	1956	1960	1964	1968	1972	1976	1980	1984	1988	1992	1996	2000	2004	2008	2012

RAFER'S RUN FOR THE GOLD

1960 ROME, ITALY

Rafer Johnson and C. K. Yang were good friends as well as teammates at the University of California, Los Angeles, in the 1950s. But during the Olympics, the two decathletes were

A natural athlete with great self-confidence, Rafer Johnson decided at 16 years old to do the decathlon

competitors. Johnson represented the United States. Yang was from Taiwan.

The decathlon is a grueling, 10-event competition held over just 2 days, and the Olympic winner typically is awarded the title of "world's greatest athlete." The events include the 100-meter dash, long jump, shot put, high jump, 400-meter dash, 110-meter hurdles, discus, pole vault, javelin, and 1,500-meter run. Johnson won the silver medal during the 1956 Olympics in Melbourne, Australia. In 1960 in Rome, Italy, Johnson and Yang were two of the favorites to win gold.

On the first day of competition, Johnson and Yang were atop the leaderboard, just as everyone expected. They traded first and second place throughout a dreary, rainy day. That first night, Johnson held a slim, 55-point lead over his friend (scoring charts are used to determine decathlon points, and thousands are at stake). "Rafe and I loved competing against each other," Yang later said. "We needed each other, in a way."

The second day of the decathlon was just as close. Johnson and Yang again traded leads, and after 9 events, Johnson maintained a 67-point advantage. That was hardly safe, since the final event, the 1,500, was Yang's best race. Johnson looked at the point tables and did some math before the run. He calculated that he needed to finish the nearly 1-mile-long run within 10 seconds of Yang in order to win the gold medal. That was no easy task, though. Johnson's best time in the 1,500 was 18 seconds slower than Yang's personal record.

As difficult as it was, Johnson stayed close to Yang throughout the race. On the last lap, Yang tried to sprint away from his rival, but he just couldn't shake him. "I stuck to him like a shadow," Johnson said. When it ended, Johnson had run the fastest 1,500 of his life, coming in just 1.2 seconds behind Yang. The close, second-place finish was enough to give him 8,392 total points—58 more than Yang.

Exhausted, Johnson put his arm around Yang and rested his head on his friend's shoulder. Even though he had clinched the gold medal, Johnson also felt for Yang. "I was exhilarated that I won and totally depressed that C. K. lost," said Johnson. "I had both feelings."

When it ended, Johnson had run the fastest 1,500 of his life....

Johnson had a huge shot put in 1960, launching the shot almost three feet farther than any other decathlete

ATHENS, GREECE — 1896
PARIS, FRANCE — 1900
ST. LOUIS, MISSOURI — 1904
LONDON, ENGLAND — 1908
STOCKHOLM, SWEDEN — 1912
ANTWERP, BELGIUM — 1920
PARIS, FRANCE — 1924
AMSTERDAM, NETHERLANDS — 1928
LOS ANGELES, CALIFORNIA — 1932
BERLIN, GERMANY — 1936
LONDON, ENGLAND — 1948
HELSINKI, FINLAND — 1952
MELBOURNE, AUSTRALIA — 1956
ROME, ITALY — 1960
TOKYO, JAPAN — 1964
MEXICO CITY, MEXICO — 1968
MUNICH, WEST GERMANY — 1972
MONTREAL, QUEBEC — 1976
MOSCOW, SOVIET UNION — 1980
LOS ANGELES, CALIFORNIA — 1984
SEOUL, SOUTH KOREA — 1988
BARCELONA, SPAIN — 1992
ATLANTA, GEORGIA — 1996
SYDNEY, AUSTRALIA — 2000
ATHENS, GREECE — 2004
BEIJING, CHINA — 2008
LONDON, ENGLAND — 2012

BEAMON TAKES FLIGHT

1968   MEXICO CITY, MEXICO

Between the years 1935 and 1968, the world record for the long jump improved by a mere eight and a half inches. In 1935, the great Jesse Owens jumped 26 feet, 8-1/4 inches, and no one improved on that mark until 1960, when rivals Ralph Boston of the U.S. and Igor Ter-Ovanesyan

It took a superhuman leap by Mike Powell (above) to surpass Bob Beamon's historic 1968 jump (opposite)

of the Soviet Union began stretching the tape bit by bit until it reached 27 feet, 4-¾ inches.

But American jumper Bob Beamon changed everything on October 18, 1968, in Mexico City. On that day, Beamon jumped 29 feet, 2-½ inches, beating the previous record by an incredible 21-¾ inches—nearly 2 feet! It was a leap that stretched beyond the imagination of even the best long jumpers. Englishman Lynn Davies, who had won gold in the long jump in the 1964 Games in Tokyo, told Beamon, "You have destroyed this event."

The 6-foot-3 and 160-pound Beamon didn't realize what he had done at first. When he landed in the sand, he bounced three times on his way out of the pit and jogged back to a bench to wait for the measurement. "It felt like a regular jump," he said. But others knew differently. Owens, who witnessed the jump while looking on as a radio commentator, remarked that it was a perfect jump.

It took more than 15 minutes for Beamon to find out how far he had leaped. As he waited, he suspected that he might have broken the record— but by only a bit. Officials called for a tape measure because the rail that carried the **optical** sight used for precise measurement was not long enough to scope the mark in the sand. When the official distance—8.90 meters— flashed on the scoreboard, Beamon still did not know what he had done because he did not know how that metric distance converted to feet and inches. When he was finally told his distance, Beamon was so overcome with disbelief that he collapsed on the track. Boston told him that the competition was all but over, and Ter-Ovanesyan said, "Compared to that jump, the rest of us are just children." Beamon's world record stood for almost 23 years before it was broken by American Mike Powell. However, as of 2011, it remained the Olympic record.

ATHENS, GREECE | 1896
PARIS, FRANCE | 1900
ST. LOUIS, MISSOURI | 1904
LONDON, ENGLAND | 1908
STOCKHOLM, SWEDEN | 1912
ANTWERP, BELGIUM | 1920
PARIS, FRANCE | 1924
AMSTERDAM, NETHERLANDS | 1928
LOS ANGELES, CALIFORNIA | 1932
BERLIN, GERMANY | 1936
LONDON, ENGLAND | 1948
HELSINKI, FINLAND | 1952
MELBOURNE, AUSTRALIA | 1956
ROME, ITALY | 1960
TOKYO, JAPAN | 1964
MEXICO CITY, MEXICO | 1968
MUNICH, WEST GERMANY | 1972
MONTREAL, QUEBEC | 1976
MOSCOW, SOVIET UNION | 1980
LOS ANGELES, CALIFORNIA | 1984
SEOUL, SOUTH KOREA | 1988
BARCELONA, SPAIN | 1992
ATLANTA, GEORGIA | 1996
SYDNEY, AUSTRALIA | 2000
ATHENS, GREECE | 2004
BEIJING, CHINA | 2008
LONDON, ENGLAND | 2012

KING CARL

CARL LEWIS U.S. EVENTS: 100-METER DASH, 200-METER DASH, LONG JUMP,

4X100-METER RELAY OLYMPIC COMPETITIONS: 1984, 1988, 1992, 1996

With nine gold medals over the span of four Olympics, it's difficult to pinpoint the greatest moment of Carl Lewis's career. It could be the four golds the sprinter and jumper won in 1984 in Los Angeles, California, matching the feat of his hero Jesse Owens from nearly 50 years earlier. It could be the four consecutive golds he won in the long jump, tying a record set by discus thrower Al Oerter in the 1950s and '60s.

Perhaps the greatness of Lewis's career is truly in the sum of its parts. After all, only one other track-and-field athlete, Paavo Nurmi, and three other Olympians have had nine gold medals hung around their

The nine gold medals of Carl Lewis (second from left) prompted the IOC to vote him "Sportsman of the Century"

necks. "He was the Babe Ruth and Michael Jordan of our sport," said U.S. track and field spokesman Pete Cava, comparing Lewis to the greatest baseball and basketball players of all time.

Lewis might have won more medals had the U.S. not **boycotted** the 1980 Olympics in Moscow, Soviet Union, for political reasons. In 1984, when he finally got his chance, he dominated the Games. The 23-year-old won the 100-meter dash, set an Olympic record in the 200 meters, and helped the American 4x100-meter relay team to a world-record win. Some people thought Lewis might break Bob Beamon's long jump world record. He didn't, but he still

Carl Lewis's Gold Medals

Los Angeles, 1984	100–meter dash
	200–meter dash
	4x100 relay
	Long jump
Seoul, 1988	100–meter dash
	Long jump
Barcelona, 1992	4x100 relay
	Long jump
Atlanta, 1996	Long jump

outjumped the competition by nearly a foot.

In 1988 in Seoul, South Korea, Lewis ran the 100 in world-record time, but he was beaten to the finish line by Canada's Ben Johnson. However, Lewis ended up with gold when Johnson failed a test for **steroids** and was disqualified and stripped of his medal. Lewis also won a gold medal in the long jump and a silver in the 200 that year.

After Lewis won in the long jump and the 4x100 relay in 1992 in Barcelona, Spain, many people thought he would end his career with eight gold medals. When the 1996 Games took place in Atlanta, Georgia, Lewis was 35 years old—no longer a young athlete like most of his competitors. But he took to the long jump seeking one last moment of glory. He **fouled** on his first jump and was in third place after his second. But on his third try, Lewis flew through the air and landed 27 feet, 10-3/4 inches from where he took off. It was his best jump in two years, and it was good enough to win his fourth gold medal in the event. "You've just seen a great performer at the end of his career," said Lewis's coach, Tom Tellez. "People thought he couldn't do it, but he did. He's the greatest athlete I've ever seen."

Lewis may have been an even better jumper than sprinter, dominating the long jump for a decade

ATHENS, GREECE	PARIS, FRANCE	ST. LOUIS, MISSOURI	LONDON, ENGLAND	STOCKHOLM, SWEDEN	ANTWERP, BELGIUM	PARIS, FRANCE	AMSTERDAM, NETHERLANDS	LOS ANGELES, CALIFORNIA	BERLIN, GERMANY	LONDON, ENGLAND	HELSINKI, FINLAND	MELBOURNE, AUSTRALIA	ROME, ITALY	TOKYO, JAPAN	MEXICO CITY, MEXICO	MUNICH, WEST GERMANY	MONTREAL, QUEBEC	MOSCOW, SOVIET UNION	LOS ANGELES, CALIFORNIA	SEOUL, SOUTH KOREA	BARCELONA, SPAIN	ATLANTA, GEORGIA	SYDNEY, AUSTRALIA	ATHENS, GREECE	BEIJING, CHINA	LONDON, ENGLAND			
1896	1900	1904	1908	1912	1920	1924	1928	1932	1936	1948	1952	1956	1960	1964	1968	1972	1976	1980	1984	1988	1992	1996	2000	2004	2008	2012			

QUEEN OF THE TRACK

JACKIE JOYNER-KERSEE U.S. EVENTS: HEPTATHLON, LONG JUMP

OLYMPIC COMPETITIONS: 1984, 1988, 1992, 1996

When it comes to track and field, many athletes are good at one discipline. But multi-event athletes must be good at several different sports. Their muscles have to be trained to sprint, run, jump, and throw at high levels. Jackie Joyner-Kersee wasn't just good at those things, she

From the high jump (above) to the shot put (opposite), Jackie Joyner-Kersee seemed to have no weakness

was exceptional. "She's the greatest multi-sport athlete, man or woman," said American Bruce Jenner, who won the gold medal in the decathlon in 1976.

Joyner-Kersee competed in the heptathlon, a grueling 2-day event that includes 7 disciplines—the 100-meter hurdles, high jump, shot put, 200-meter dash, long jump, javelin, and 800-meter run. Like the men's decathlon, points are given for results, and no competitor scored more points than Jackie. She was the first ever to score more than 7,000 points in the event.

In 1984 in Los Angeles, California, Joyner-Kersee missed gold by just five points. Settling for the silver medal was tough, considering that the only difference between silver and gold was just a fraction of a second in the 800. But she handled it with class and with a smile on her face. That cheerful sportsmanship would endear her to fans for the next three Olympics.

In Seoul, South Korea, Joyner-Kersee had her moment. She dominated, taking first place in four of the seven events and second in another to score a world-record 7,291 points for her first gold medal. Overcoming sore knees, aching muscles, and **asthma** that made breathing

difficult, she won the heptathlon gold again in 1992 in Barcelona, Spain. "Her performances are like a great opera or concert," said her coach and husband, Bob Kersee. "I feel like I should be wearing a tux when I watch them."

The long jump was one of Joyner-Kersee's best events. Her jumping ability not only helped her in the heptathlon, but also gave her more medals. She won the gold medal in the long jump in 1988, becoming the first woman to win multi-event and individual-event championships in the same Olympics. Joyner-Kersee finished her Olympic career with six medals, more track-and-field medals than any other American woman as of 2011. "She is inspiration," said American sprinter Gail Devers. "She is to be admired. She's beauty. She's grace. She is called the first lady of track and field for a reason."

ATHENS, GREECE
PARIS, FRANCE
ST. LOUIS, MISSOURI
LONDON, ENGLAND
STOCKHOLM, SWEDEN
ANTWERP, BELGIUM
PARIS, FRANCE
AMSTERDAM, NETHERLANDS
LOS ANGELES, CALIFORNIA
BERLIN, GERMANY
LONDON, ENGLAND
HELSINKI, FINLAND
MELBOURNE, AUSTRALIA
ROME, ITALY
TOKYO, JAPAN
MEXICO CITY, MEXICO
MUNICH, WEST GERMANY
MONTREAL, QUEBEC
MOSCOW, SOVIET UNION
LOS ANGELES, CALIFORNIA
SEOUL, SOUTH KOREA
BARCELONA, SPAIN
ATLANTA, GEORGIA
SYDNEY, AUSTRALIA
ATHENS, GREECE
BEIJING, CHINA
LONDON, ENGLAND

1896 1900 1904 1908 1912 1920 1924 1928 1932 1936 1948 1952 1956 1960 1964 1968 1972 1976 1980 1984 1988 **1992** 1996 2000 2004 2008 2012

THE COURAGE TO FINISH

1992 BARCELONA, SPAIN

When he was 19 years old, Derek Redmond was the best 400-meter runner in Great Britain, setting his country's record in the event. His next goal was to win a medal in the Olympics. But Redmond had some bad luck in Seoul, South Korea, in 1988, withdrawing from the competition

Derek Redmond's career was undermined by injuries, but his emotional lap in 1992 will never be forgotten

at the last minute due to an **Achilles tendon** injury. He would have to wait four years to try again.

In 1992 in Barcelona, Spain, Redmond was ready to go and feeling good. Just a year earlier, he had broken the national record he had set in 1987. Running in the Olympic semifinals, he got off to a great start and appeared to be sprinting his way to a spot in the 400 finals. But just past the midway point of the race, halfway around the track, Redmond heard a pop and felt a stabbing pain in the back of his right leg. He immediately grabbed the back of his thigh and went down on the track. He thought he had been shot. The reality was not as severe but nearly as painful—he had torn his **hamstring**. His hope for a medal was gone.

After all the other runners had completed the race, Redmond decided that he wanted to finish, too. He got up and began to limp and hobble around the track on the strength of his one good leg. "I would have laid there," said that year's British track captain, Linford Christie. "There's no way I would have got up because when you've got a hamstring [tear], you know you've got a hamstring."

As the injured Redmond made the final turn, a man came out of the cheering crowd and ran onto the track to Redmond. It was his father, Jim. Jim Redmond put one arm around his son and took his hand. Derek was in tears and buried his face in his father's shoulder as Jim brushed away security and medical staff. Jim told his son that he didn't have to finish the race, that he had nothing left to prove, but Derek insisted on making it all the way around. "Whatever happens, he had to finish," Jim said, "and I was there to help him finish."

ATHENS, GREECE
PARIS, FRANCE
ST. LOUIS, MISSOURI
LONDON, ENGLAND
STOCKHOLM, SWEDEN
ANTWERP, BELGIUM
PARIS, FRANCE
AMSTERDAM, NETHERLANDS
LOS ANGELES, CALIFORNIA
BERLIN, GERMANY
LONDON, ENGLAND
HELSINKI, FINLAND
MELBOURNE, AUSTRALIA
ROME, ITALY
TOKYO, JAPAN
MEXICO CITY, MEXICO
MUNICH, WEST GERMANY
MONTREAL, QUEBEC
MOSCOW, SOVIET UNION
LOS ANGELES, CALIFORNIA
SEOUL, SOUTH KOREA
BARCELONA, SPAIN
ATLANTA, GEORGIA
SYDNEY, AUSTRALIA
ATHENS, GREECE
BEIJING, CHINA
LONDON, ENGLAND

1896 1900 1904 1908 1912 1920 1924 1928 1932 1936 1948 1952 1956 1960 1964 1968 1972 1976 1980 1984 1988 1992 1996 2000 2004 2008 2012

JOHNSON PULLS OFF THE DOUBLE

1996 ATLANTA, GEORGIA

Michael Johnson felt the pressure. He wanted to feel the pressure. Eighty thousand people filled the Centennial Olympic Stadium in Atlanta, Georgia, and most of them were there to see

Michael Johnson made the 1996 Games his personal showcase, claiming two golds and a world record

him make history on that August evening. "I wish more people thought I couldn't do it," he said. "The higher the stakes, the better I am."

Camera flashes popped all around the track as Johnson loosened up in his lane before attempting to become the first man to win the 200- and 400-meter dashes in the same Olympic Games. He had already accomplished half of his goal, dominating the 400 in an Olympic-record time of 43.49 seconds.

Johnson actually put a lot of the pressure on himself. Before the Olympics, the American sprinter requested that the traditional track schedule be changed to allow him the chance to attempt the double. Instead of running the two events over two days, the two finals took place three days apart. Johnson also unveiled a pair of golden Nike track shoes for his races. He knew that the spikes would look silly on someone who failed to win a gold medal.

When it came time to run the 200-meter final, Johnson's body was sore from the previous seven races, including preliminaries and the 400 final. But Johnson wasn't going to let the pain keep him down. Running with a straight-up style that drew comparisons to the great Jesse Owens, Johnson got a good start when the gun fired. And as he rounded the turn and hit the straightaway, he rocketed past the rest of the field, widening his lead with each stride. When Johnson hit the finish line, he turned to his left to peek at his time. When he saw it— 19.32 seconds—he dropped his jaw and stretched out his arms in both celebration and disbelief. Johnson had broken his own world record by .34 seconds, a seemingly impossible leap. "I am rarely shocked by my own performance," Johnson said. "And I am shocked."

Johnson's act in Atlanta didn't just make history. It changed the way people thought of sprinting. Traditionally, the winner of the men's 100-meter dash is considered the fastest human in the world. But after Michael Johnson's unforgettable 200, many people thought that title should go to him.

> **"I am rarely shocked by my own performance. And I am shocked."**
>
> – *Michael Johnson*

ATHENS, GREECE 1896 · PARIS, FRANCE 1900 · ST. LOUIS, MISSOURI 1904 · LONDON, ENGLAND 1908 · STOCKHOLM, SWEDEN 1912 · ANTWERP, BELGIUM 1920 · PARIS, FRANCE 1924 · AMSTERDAM, NETHERLANDS 1928 · LOS ANGELES, CALIFORNIA 1932 · BERLIN, GERMANY 1936 · LONDON, ENGLAND 1948 · HELSINKI, FINLAND 1952 · MELBOURNE, AUSTRALIA 1956 · ROME, ITALY 1960 · TOKYO, JAPAN 1964 · MEXICO CITY, MEXICO 1968 · MUNICH, WEST GERMANY 1972 · MONTREAL, QUEBEC 1976 · MOSCOW, SOVIET UNION 1980 · LOS ANGELES, CALIFORNIA 1984 · SEOUL, SOUTH KOREA 1988 · BARCELONA, SPAIN 1992 · ATLANTA, GEORGIA 1996 · SYDNEY, AUSTRALIA 2000 · ATHENS, GREECE 2004 · **BEIJING, CHINA 2008** · LONDON, ENGLAND 2012

HOW MUCH FASTER?

2008 BEIJING, CHINA

Usain Bolt had the perfect last name for an Olympic sprinter. In 2008, in Beijing, China, the Jamaican was as fast as lightning, winning the 100-meter dash. He ran the race in 9.69 seconds, a world-record time some experts predicted wouldn't be seen for at least another 20 years. "It no longer is good enough to be sub-10 [seconds]," TV commentator and Olympic medalist Ato Boldon

With his towering frame and blistering speed, Usain Bolt was the star of the Beijing Games track events

Bolt crushed the 2008 field in the 100-meter dash by a margin seldom seen in the event's history

said. "They have now gone into the realm of video-game times…. and [Bolt] made it look easy."

It was so easy for Bolt that, with 15 meters remaining in the race, he began to celebrate the incredible victory. The 6-foot-5 sprinter reached out his long arms, looked up into the crowd of 90,000 that filled the National Stadium, and began to pound his chest. As he did so, he decelerated. He was not running his fastest when he crossed the finish line, still well ahead of silver medalist Richard Thompson of Trinidad and Tobago and bronze medalist Walter Dix of the U.S.

Some people thought that Bolt showed poor sportsmanship by celebrating before the race had ended. But almost everyone wondered: How much faster could he have gone had he not slowed down? The winner of the 100 meters gets the unofficial title of "world's fastest human," and Boldon figured Bolt wasted a chance to run the race in 9.59 seconds and make that title his for years to come.

The 21-year-old Bolt, however, didn't seem to care about the time. He was already the world record holder before the Olympics began. "Not important," he said. "I had the record, I still have it. Now I have the gold medal, too."

Bolt won two other gold medals in Beijing. He set another world record in the 200 meters, which was considered his best event, finishing that race in 19.30 seconds. He also helped the Jamaican team capture the 4x100 relay world record with a time of 37.10 seconds. A year later at the world championships in Berlin, Germany, Bolt ran all the way through the tape and lowered his world record to an incredible 9.58 seconds. "What can you say?" American sprinter Darvis Patton said of Bolt. "He's a freak of nature. He's like [basketball stars Michael] Jordan and LeBron [James], in a league of his own."

Until Bolt arrived, the 100-meter world record usually was lowered by mere hundredths of a second

ATHENS, GREECE — 1896
PARIS, FRANCE — 1900
ST. LOUIS, MISSOURI — 1904
LONDON, ENGLAND — 1908
STOCKHOLM, SWEDEN — 1912
ANTWERP, BELGIUM — 1920
PARIS, FRANCE — 1924
AMSTERDAM, NETHERLANDS — 1928
LOS ANGELES, CALIFORNIA — 1932
BERLIN, GERMANY — 1936
LONDON, ENGLAND — 1948
HELSINKI, FINLAND — 1952
MELBOURNE, AUSTRALIA — 1956
ROME, ITALY — 1960
TOKYO, JAPAN — 1964
MEXICO CITY, MEXICO — 1968
MUNICH, WEST GERMANY — 1972
MONTREAL, QUEBEC — 1976
MOSCOW, SOVIET UNION — 1980
LOS ANGELES, CALIFORNIA — 1984
SEOUL, SOUTH KOREA — 1988
BARCELONA, SPAIN — 1992
ATLANTA, GEORGIA — 1996
SYDNEY, AUSTRALIA — 2000
ATHENS, GREECE — 2004
BEIJING, CHINA — 2008
LONDON, ENGLAND — 2012

THE GAMES OF 2012

The 2012 Olympics were to be held in London, England. Londoners got the news in July 2005, and as is the case any time an Olympic host is selected, city and national officials sprang into action. Although seven years may seem to be plenty of time for preparation, it is in fact a small window when one considers that host cities typically need to create housing for thousands of

In 2012, London was to play host to its third Summer Olympiad, having done so in 1908 and 1948

international athletes and coaches (generally in a consolidated area known as the "Athletes' Village"), expand public transportation options (such as trains and buses), and build outdoor playing fields, indoor arenas, and other venues with enough seating—and grandeur—to be worthy of Olympic competition.

The numbers involved in the 2012 Games indicate just how large a venture it is to host an Olympiad. Some 10,500 athletes from 200 countries were to compete in London, with 2,100 medals awarded. About 8 million tickets were expected to be sold for the Games. And before any athletes arrived or any medals were awarded, it was anticipated that the total cost of London's Olympics-related building projects and other preparations would approach $15 billion.

Among those construction projects was the creation of Olympic Park, a sprawling gathering area in east London that was to function as a center of activity during the Games. From the park, people would be able to move to numerous athletic facilities in and around the city. Those facilities included the 80,000-seat Olympic Stadium, which was built to host track

and field events as well as the opening and closing ceremonies; the new Basketball Arena, a temporary structure that was to be dismantled after the Games; and the $442-million Aquatics Centre, which was designed both to host swimming events and to serve as a kind of visitors' gateway to Olympic Park. Other notable venues included the North Greenwich Arena (which was to host gymnastics), the ExCeL center (boxing), Earls Court (indoor volleyball), and Horse Guards Parade (beach volleyball).

In July 2011, British prime minister David Cameron and IOC president Jacques Rogge reviewed all preparations and proudly declared that the city was nearly ready to welcome the world. "This has the makings of a great British success story," Cameron announced. "With a year to go, it's on time, it's on budget.... We must offer the greatest ever Games in the world's greatest country."

Rogge kicked off the one-year countdown to the Games by formally inviting countries around the world to send their greatest athletes to the British capital in 2012. "The athletes will be ready," said Rogge. "And so will London."

Achilles tendon — a strong length of tissue that joins the muscles of a person's lower leg to the bone of the heel

asthma — a condition of the lungs that can cause wheezing and coughing and makes it difficult for a person to breathe

auxiliaries — people or groups who provide outside assistance or extra power

boycotted — protested or showed disapproval of something by refusing to participate in an event

cartilage — a strong but flexible material found in certain parts of the body that protects joints by preventing bones from grinding against each other

cinder — burned or partially burned substances, such as coal or wood; years ago, running tracks were covered with fine cinders

disciplines — particular athletic events within a larger sport

discuses — heavy, flat, round objects that are thrown in competition; men throw a discus weighing 4.4 pounds, and women throw one weighing 2.2 pounds

fouled — committed a sports infraction, typically by exceeding a boundary line

führer — a tyrannical leader; the title adopted by German dictator Adolf Hitler

gait — a particular way of walking or running

hamstring — the muscles and tendons in the back of the upper leg

heat — in track, one of multiple preliminary races used to determine the field for the final medal competition

javelins — long, spear-like objects that are thrown in competition; men throw a javelin that is at least 102.4 inches long, and women throw one that is at least 86.6 inches long

leg — one athlete's section of a team relay race; in a relay, athletes pass a cylinder called a baton to teammates as one leg ends and another begins

memento — something that is kept as a reminder of a person, place, or thing

optical — relating to a device used to help a person see

Pop Warner — a college football coach in the late 1800s and early 1900s who won four national championships and made many important innovations to the game

qualifying rounds — early races or competitions that eliminate some athletes and move others closer to the finals

shot put — an event in which athletes throw a large, heavy, metal ball called a shot; men throw a 16-pound shot, while women throw an 8.8-pound shot

steeplechase — a 3,000-meter track race that features several obstacles, including water jumps and barriers similar to hurdles

steroids — chemical substances or drugs that affect muscle growth; some athletes have used them illegally to become stronger and faster

Windsor Castle — one of the official residences of the British king or queen, located about 20 miles west of London, England

Selected Bibliography

Cousineau, Phil. *The Olympic Odyssey: Rekindling the True Spirit of the Great Games.* Wheaton, Ill.: The Theosophical Publishing House, 2003.

Hoffer, Richard. "Our Favorite Feats." *Sports Illustrated,* December 27, 1999.

Layden, Tim. "Faster than Fast." *Sports Illustrated,* August 25, 2008.

MacCambridge, Michael, ed. *SportsCentury.* New York: ESPN, 1999.

Macy, Sue, and Bob Costas. *Swifter, Higher, Stronger: A Photographic History of the Summer Olympics.* Washington, D.C.: National Geographic, 2008.

Maraniss, David. *Rome 1960: The Olympics that Changed the World.* New York: Simon & Schuster, 2008.

Moore, Kenny. "Triumph and Tragedy in Los Angeles." *Sports Illustrated,* August 20, 1984.

The New York Times. "Hayes, American, Marathon Winner." July 24, 1908.

Web Sites

International Olympic Committee
www.olympic.org
This site is the official online home of the Olympics and features profiles of athletes, overviews of every sport, coverage of preparation for the 2012 Summer Games, and more.

Sports-Reference / Olympic Sports
www.sports-reference.com/olympics
This site is a comprehensive database for Olympic sports and features complete facts and statistics from all Olympic Games, including medal counts, Olympic records, and more.

INDEX

Published by Creative Education
P.O. Box 227, Mankato, Minnesota 56002
Creative Education is an imprint of
The Creative Company
www.thecreativecompany.us

Design and production by The Design Lab
Art direction by Rita Marshall

Printed by Corporate Graphics in
the United States of America

Photographs by Alamy (ACE STOCK LIMITED,
Daily Mail/Rex, Everett Collection Inc,
INTERFOTO, Diane Johnson, Lou Linwei,
M&N, Photos 12, Pictorial Press Ltd), American
Numismatic Society, Dreamstime (Alain Lacroix),
Getty Images (Getty Images, IOC/Allsport, JEFF
HAYNES/AFP, JOHN MACDOUGALL/AFP, Gray
Mortimore /Allsport, Hy Peskin/Sports Illustrated,
Popperfoto, Mike Powell /Allsport, Topical Press
Agency), iStockphoto (Ken Brown, Marisa Allegra
Williams), Shutterstock (Pete Niesen)

Library of Congress
Cataloging-in-Publication Data
Frederick, Shane.
Track and field / by Shane Frederick.
p. cm. — (Summer Olympic legends)
Includes bibliographical references and index.
Summary: A survey of the highlights and
legendary athletes—such as Jamaican Usain
Bolt—of the Olympic sport of track and field,
which has been part of the modern Summer
Games since 1896.
ISBN 978-1-60818-212-1
1. Track and field athletes—Biography—Juvenile
literature. 2. Track and field—Juvenile literature.
3. Olympics—Juvenile literature. I. Title.
GV697.A1F688 2012
796.420922—dc23 [B]   2011032498

CPSIA: 030111 PO 1452

First Edition
9 8 7 6 5 4 3 2 1